The Process of Change Interactive Workbook

Love Yourself: Volume Two

Precious Brown

The Process of Change
Love Yourself: Volume Two
Copyright © 2015 by Precious Brown

All rights are reserved. Except as permitted under the U.S. Copyright Act of 1976, no part of the publication may be reproduced, distributed or transmitted in any form or by any means, or stored in a database or retrieval system without the prior written permission of the publisher.

This book is available in volume for qualifying organizations.

Please contact the author to inquire at
admin@choosingourdecisionseveryday.com.

All definitions, unless otherwise indicated, are taken from merriam-webster.com ®, Copyright© 2015.

For more information about this book, coaching, or speaking engagements please visit www.changenegative2positive.com or email admin@choosingourdecisionseveryday.com.

Flint Michigan
Since 2015

ISBN 978-0996134729
For Worldwide Distribution
Printed in the U.S.A

Contents

Dedication
Introduction

1. What Is Love?
2. How Do I Love Myself?
3. Accept Yourself As You Are
4. Embrace Your Individualism
5. Be Honest With Yourself
6. Forgive Yourself
7. Respect Yourself
8. Build Your Character
9. Spend Time With Yourself
10. Love Yourself Enough
11. Love
12. Love Quotes

Dedication

I dedicate this book to my heavenly father, God and my earthly father, Cloyd Kilgore Jr.

God, I thank You for Your agape love. The kind of love that is absolute, undeserving and unconditional. It is because of that love I have learned to love my enemies, family and friends without question and regardless of circumstance.

I thank You for loving me when I didn't know how to love myself. I thank You for sending me an angel in disguise, Cloyd Kilgore. I thank You for giving me a second chance to live life and live it according to Your will. It is only by Your grace and mercy that I am sober with a sound mind.

As such, I am willing and able to create this workbook for the betterment of Your people. I believe it is Your will for me to share my testimonies so others will be freed from bondage.

To my earthly father, I thank you for loving me in spite of me and through it all. You are an inspiration to me. You have been teaching me the lesson of love my entire life and for that I am grateful.

As a child I did not understand the fullness of your teachings and yet you continued to teach. I am pleased to tell you, *"I get it now."* Thank you from the bottom of my heart for your determination and persistence. It is because of you this dream never died.

Introduction

Throughout my change process I have realized one of the most challenging tasks in my life was to genuinely love myself. To my surprise, when speaking with others, many have had this same problem. I became enthralled on a journey to fully understand and explain what it means to love yourself.

In this volume of the series you will be challenged to begin the *Love Yourself* process. I encourage you to take your time when reading and completing the journal writings. It will be to your advantage to revisit the sections of the book often, especially when dealing with different areas in your life. The listed techniques are provided to assist you with implementing the process of loving yourself.

Remember to keep an open mind and remain focused. There is no order for the techniques to be used so feel free to jump around based on what issue you are addressing in life.

The hierarchy of love in our lives should be to love God, yourself and then love others.

Over time – and through all the hurts and pains of life – you may have lost the innocent love you once had. Until this stage of your change process, you may not have noticed it was gone. Nonetheless, it is. The important thing is you are willing to try and regain the love within that has dwindled. To attain this goal you must learn to genuinely love yourself before you are able to love anyone else. This book is a guide to assist you with loving yourself and loving others.

Everything in life is a process and love is no different. In this process you will be challenged to do more self-checking. You will be required to evaluate the love you have for yourself and how you love others. Once you complete the steps to implement techniques of self-love, you will then be able to move forward and deal with how to love others.

This book will force you to embrace your negatives and change them into positives. Every time you recognize a negative emotion or thought, allow yourself to stop and deal with it. Journal it, accept it and move on. Our emotions and thoughts are our internal experiences that make up who we are so we must deal with them. Accepting our negatives (problems) as chances to change can provide positive results (problem solving).

This process is not instantaneous or automatic. It will cause you to do more digging within and create more changes in your life. It may prove to be difficult and sometimes uncomfortable, but it will help you. I encourage you to stay the course, dig deeper within and prepare yourself for more positive changes in your life.

You have taken another brave and needed step in your life. I applaud you for continuing to the next phase of your change process.

PREPARE YOURSELF FOR MORE POSITIVE LIFE CHANGES

What Is Love?

Throughout life there have been many aspects of love displayed. There is parental, sibling, couple, and friendship aspects to name a few. In each relationship the definition and boundary of love changes based upon the individuals involved.

Per **Webster's dictionary love is defined as** *(1)*: strong affection for another arising out of kinship or personal ties <maternal *love* for a child> *(2)*: attraction based on sexual desire: affection and tenderness felt by lovers *(3)*: affection based on admiration, benevolence, or common interests <*love* for his old schoolmates>. The definition of Love is great! But the truth is until you can define what love means to you, no other definition matters.

For the purposes of this book we define Love in the simplest of terms: an affection for someone. Would you be inclined to agree that you are **someone**? If so, that means you are supposed to love yourself. Yet, when we think of loving someone we seem to neglect ourselves. We are busy trying to love everyone and everything around us and take no time to learn how to love ourselves.

I can admit, at one time in my life, I did not know how to love myself nor did I know how to start. Can you be that honest? I hope so because these are the type of journal writings you will deal with in this workbook.

Regardless of what you have ever been told or overheard; **you are someone and you deserve to love yourself**. So let's get to work and expect greater changes. We will start with the foundation question *"What does love mean to you?"* Although there are many ways to answer this question, it is of utmost importance that you focus on: **what you feel or think love is versus what someone else told you it is or should be.** Take a minute and really ponder what love is to you?

Writing #1

- ✓ Write your definition of love.
- ✓ Write how you apply it to your life (exclude material things).
- ✓ Write new ways you can display self-love.

_____
_____
_____
_____
_____
_____
_____
_____
_____
_____
_____
_____

How Do I Love Myself?

This is my *"open my eyes"* question. I had to ask myself this question one day. I clearly understood I wanted other people to love me, but how could they when I did not know how to love me? I pondered this question for months. It was a critical piece of my life's puzzle, which was not fitting. It was a crushing blow when I realized *"I did not know how to love myself."* Thus, the journaling and searching began.

Be patient with yourself. Patience is definitely a skill learned over time. In our "right now" society it is almost impossible to be patient for anything. However, I encourage you to hone this skill. It is not going to be easy, especially if you are impatient like I was. Simply put, patience, in this instance, is **giving yourself time to change**.

Although there may be several reasons why we are impatient with ourselves, I believe the main one is because we want to see this great progress. But, we don't have the time to wait for it. You did not get to this point in life overnight nor **will** you be able to change overnight. Honestly, this is still a test for me from time to time.

When I began to journal the techniques for this workbook I wanted everything to be completed instantly. I felt as if the words were supposed to arrange themselves on the paper or in my computer so I could get this great end product for you all to see.

After a few starts, stops and a lot of frustration, I wanted to quit. Instead, I walked away from it. I waited a few days, got some rest and started fresh and my thoughts began to flow. At that point, I knew I was being impatient by rushing myself. I had to acknowledge the root of the impatience. When you begin to get impatient about your change process ask yourself, ***"What's the rush?"***

Writing #2

- ✓ Write two positive changes you have made since starting your process of change.
- ✓ Write how long you engaged in the negative behavior prior to the change.
- ✓ Treat yourself for the accomplishment.

_____

_____

_____

_____

_____

_____

_____

_____

_____

_____

_____

Accept Yourself As You Are!

Acceptance is key. Accept who you are and where you are in life. Self-acceptance allows you to be free. Own who you are. You must get to a point of being okay with yourself regardless of the circumstance or situation. You must understand who you are and who you want to be.

To be successful in accepting yourself it is important that you conquer the following tasks:

- **Let go of the past.** You cannot change or fix it. You can only learn from it and move on.
- **Do not try to be perfect.** We all do it in our own way, consciously or unconsciously, in many areas of our lives. Remember no one is perfect. You are allowed to make mistakes, just try not to repeat them.
- **Do not compare yourself to others.** You are who the Creator created you to be. You are the way He created you to be. Life has happened. Accept the good and bad and

believe you are still who the Creator designed you to be, flaws and all.

- **Do not compete with others.** It is not important to keep up with the Jones'. It is not important to have the best of the best and be empty on the inside. However, it is important to be you - rich or poor, popular or not. Remember that life is a challenge, not a competition.

When I decided to write this volume of the series, I began to review myself and noticed there were things about me I still wanted to change. One of my flaws is my mouth. It is a blessing and a curse. Sometimes I just need to shut up.

I was speaking with some young ladies about dealing with issues in relationships. During the discussion one of the young ladies mentioned that she knew someone that seemed to enjoy fighting with her boyfriend. It was the way they showed their love. Instantly, I was agitated. Before I knew it I was expressing how stupid that was, and if they truly loved each other there is no way they would fight like that, and love doesn't hurt and on and on.

I never noticed how solemn the young lady began to look until I shut up. Once I did she finally said, "That's all I have known." My mouth fell open. I never thought she was speaking about herself. Had I kept my opinion to myself and allowed her to finish sharing I possibly could have helped her more.

At that point, I had accepted the fact that I do have a big mouth in combination with being opinionated. I also learned the lesson on keeping my mouth shut especially when others finally open up to share their story (or anyone else's). Now, I fully get the notion that my opinion does not always have to, nor need to, be voiced. Since then I make a conscious effort to not give an opinion if it was not requested.

Writing #3

- ✓ Write a little love note to yourself.
- ✓ Write 2-3 things that you need to accept about yourself.
- ✓ Write an acceptance letter to yourself about each thing you listed above.

_____

_____

_____

_____

_____

_____

_____

_____

_____

_____

_____

_____

Embrace Your Individualism

To fully be who you really are and truly love yourself you must be willing to acknowledge, accept and embrace everything about you – that includes attitudes, flaws, pet peeves and physical characteristics. In volume one of *The Process of Change* there is a chapter titled ***Who am I?*** It deals with identifying your likes, dislikes and pinpointing triggers in your life. The next step is to identify your uniqueness - things that make you stand out and make you different from the crowd.

This was difficult for me growing up. People around me saw my outgoing personality and fun spirit. I went the extra mile to be outgoing around others because on the inside I was broken, unhappy and I felt unworthy. I saw myself as fat and ugly. I had big lips, short hair and my legs and behind were just too big for my liking. Over time, I accepted the fact that I had low self-esteem. For this and other reasons I did not like me as a person. I did not understand the conflict in my spirit about myself.

It was not until I was a young adult did it become easier and a lot more fun in discovering my individualism. Now, I embrace all the things I once hated about myself. My lips are full to match my face. I can wear any style of hair and it is fly! Yes, I am still chunky but now that's the new skinny. I love me. All of me!

In the previous chapter I discussed one of my flaws: the big mouth. Nonetheless, in some instances it is one of my best qualities. Being vocal and sometimes outspoken has assisted me in many of my career moves. Mastering effective communication without being intimidated requires my "big mouth" sometimes. The conflict in my spirit and actions were due to my spirit wanting me to embrace who I could not see but was always there.

- ➢ Create your own style. Be unique and let your individualism flourish. Self-acceptance is not just your physical outward appearance. It is also allowing the inside of you to illuminate on the outside.

Writing #4

- ✓ List your best qualities.
- ✓ What do you like about yourself?
- ✓ What is your style?

_____

_____

_____

_____

_____

_____

_____

_____

_____

_____

_____

_____

_____

_____

Be Honest With Yourself

Honesty is the best policy if you are going to make a true change in your life. Lying to yourself only hurts you. You must be willing be honest in any situation no matter who or what it involves. Honesty will allow you to open up in your life and relationships. It will give you a sense of self-respect and others will respect you for it. It will also negate postponed hurts.

After my first marriage, I swore I would never get married again. I was bitter and hurt. I promised myself I would never let that kind of pain into my life again. Eventually, I began dating but I continuously said I had no interest in becoming a wife again. *Well, that is what I told myself.*

Not long after, I met my second husband. Over the course of six years I would run from him in hopes of not allowing myself to be hurt again. However, I knew I could not run forever. I have to admit deep down I knew I was created to be a wife. *I wanted to be a wife.* After a while I believed he was created for me.

When I finally opened up and began to be honest with myself I stopped running from him and allowed my feelings to be known. Our relationship bloomed and we were happily married. Things began to change almost immediately. I would pray for us constantly and things continued to get worse. I was lost. I didn't understand what happened. I cried out to God in despair to no avail. Finally, one day while sitting on my bed I said *"Lord, if this marriage is not for me show me"* and the lies began to unravel.

The closer we got to the end of the marriage the more I began to accept that it was over. I said to God - *"God, I'm sorry. I misunderstood what you were trying to teach me. Forgive me. Let's move on."*

The marriage lasted less than a year. As we went through the separation and divorce proceeding I noticed I was hurt but I wasn't angry or bitter. I was okay. In my prayer time I asked God *"What was that relationship about?"* In the end, my question was answered. It was revealed to me that he was in my life to teach me

I could freely love again. I was able to go through hurt and pain without completely shutting down. Praise God!

Remember, the best thing you could ever do *for* yourself is be honest *with* yourself.

Writing #5

- ✓ Write two or three things you have not been honest about with yourself.
- ✓ What keeps you from being honest with yourself about the above situations?
- ✓ Write the truth about the above situations.

_____

_____

_____

_____

_____

_____

Forgive Yourself

This is one of the most intense techniques to apply. It is not easy to forgive others and even harder to forgive yourself. The first thing you must do is allow yourself as much time as you need. Depending on the issue you may not choose to deal with it right away. Some issues cause more hurt than others. Some wounds are deeply rooted and very painful. You must keep in mind forgiveness releases you. At some point you must let go of the pain. You may not see it with your natural eye but it is killing you on the inside. The pain could be related to anger, bitterness, brokenness, love lost or withheld, family or personal sickness, trust issues, etcetera.

In volume one of *"The Process of Change"* I explained to let go is simply to acknowledge the issue, address it with the parties involved (**if applicable**), forgive and move on. It is a decision that no one can make but you.

Forgiving yourself is almost the same process. Acknowledge the issue (**whatever it is**); allow yourself to have and deal with whatever feelings you experience about the situation and move on. At this stage of your life you cannot change anything about a past situation. However, you can allow yourself to be okay with it.

This is the first time the below story will be shared with anyone. I have decided to share it with you so you fully understand the concept and importance of forgiving yourself.

In my mid-twenties I decided to terminate a pregnancy. From the moment I made the decision I began to hate myself. I knew I had no means to take care of another child but I also knew I was wrong. I felt I was stuck between a rock and a hard place. For years to come I thought about the baby often. I knew there was nothing I could do to change it but I still hated that part of me. I tried to bury the memory.

When I began to dig deep within to write *"The Process of Change"* I realized a chunk of my pain and self-hatred was due to this event in my life. It has taken over 20 years for me to forgive myself. I had to acknowledge and accept the decision I made. I allowed myself to cry out to God about it. I asked Him to forgive me and I know He has according to His word. I told myself – out loud – that I forgave me. I finally know I am okay with that decision and I am moving on. No regrets.

In life you must allow yourself to make mistakes. We all make them. If you haven't yet, keep living. You will. Learn to acknowledge them, correct them (if you can) and move on.

Writing #6

- ✓ What are two or three issues you need to apply forgiveness to in your life?
- ✓ Write a letter detailing how you feel about the issues listed in the first question.
- ✓ Write another letter giving yourself permission to release the pain from the listed issues.

Respect Yourself

Loving yourself yields a certain level of self-respect. That level of self-respect causes others to respect you. In today's society it seems that respect is no longer naturally given. Thus, it is up to you to set a boundary of respect in your life. You know how you want to be treated. You know how you want others to think of you and speak about you, especially professionally. Therefore, it is imperative that you effectively display the same level of respect toward others at all times. Key actions to create a boundary of respect are:

- **Watch your mouth!** Stop talking about people especially when you are upset. When emotions are high harmful things are said and cause situations to be worse than they truly are. On the same token be aware of your language. Be considerate enough to minimize negative and derogatory remarks. This simple act will change your atmosphere.

- **Be positive and uplifting as much as possible**. My mother always told us *"If you don't have anything nice to say, don't say anything at all."* I am ecstatic that I have learned how to apply this skill. Learn to view bad situations in a positive light. My mother and I took a trip to Indiana one day. We had taken this trip a thousand times but somehow we got on the wrong highway. It was over an hour and a half before we noticed we were going the wrong way. A four and a half hour trip turned into a seven hour trip. Now, we could have been upset, fussed and complained the rest of the trip. Not only had we wasted gas (which was $4.00 a gallon at the time). We wasted time and we got stuck in traffic. Instead we laughed and simultaneously said *"I guess God was keeping us from something we weren't supposed to be a part of."* In that instant we decided we enjoyed the scenic route. We could not change it and we were not turning around to go home so we made the best of it.

- **Stay out of other people's business**. If they do not invite you in, stay in your lane, as the saying goes. Do not offer your insight without a request. Moreover, if you are invited in, be prepared to be the listener. It is not always your place to tell someone what they should or should not do. Sometimes the person speaking may just need an ear to listen.

By implementing these three small steps people will respect you more than you can imagine.

Writing #7

- ✓ How do you define self-respect?
- ✓ How do you display self-respect?
- ✓ How can you raise your level of respect for yourself and others?
- ✓ How do you display respect for others?
- ✓ How do you display respect for people you do not particularly like?

Build Your Character

When you respect yourself you build your character. You become someone others enjoy being around. Your character affirms you. It is a statement that proceeds your every move, even when you are not present. It is who you are.

When you display negative behaviors you can surmise people will not respect you. *Why would they?* Most times you will be stereotyped and placed in a box. You must learn to apply the Golden rule: do unto others as you would want them to do unto you. You must strive to be a person of noble character. You can do it by thinking before you react, keeping your word and by being honest. Your word is your bond. Your character is your life.

In 2007, I was up for a promotion with a previous employer. I had to go through four or five interviews. My last interview was with the director. I did not know her personally nor had we ever had a conversation. After all questions were asked and answered she stated, *"Prior to us meeting I did not think you were the person for this job."*

I responded, *"Oh, really? Why not?"*

She said, *"Despite your skills, I have heard nothing but negative comments about you. I was told you were hard to work with, you are very combative and most managers do not want to deal with you. But I must admit you know your stuff."*

Then there was complete silence. I could not believe she said that to me. Nor could I believe I had been such a hard person to deal with. I felt angered inside. I wanted to give all the instances when I had been wronged. I wanted to give excuses for my behavior but instead I allowed her constructive criticism to marinate.

I went home that night and decided to build my character. I began to self-reflect. I started to see me through the eyes of others. That experience taught me the importance of my character.

Although I was rough around the edges she saw the potential. I was blessed with the promotion and the director became my mentor. Not everyone is like that. Some managers and directors would have thrown my resume in the trash and disregarded my skills. I self-reflect often and change negative behaviors as they arise.

<u>Writing #8</u>

- ✓ Ask three or four people (**not close to you**) to describe your character. Write their responses.
- ✓ What are some attributes of your character?
- ✓ Do you have character flaws that need to be corrected?
- ✓ What are you willing to change?

_____

_____

_____

_____

_____

Spend Time With Yourself - Date Yourself

When learning to love yourself you will not need a partner in crime or a tag-a-long. What you will need time. Schedule time to be by yourself. Do something that increases your awareness of love, joy and peace with yourself.

Try to do things you would not normally do. Yet, do what you love. Make yourself happy. Go to a movie, take a walk, read a book, get a massage, go to dinner or sit in silence. Do whatever makes you content within your soul! Start by scheduling your date time monthly. As time goes on you may want to increase it. It is totally up to you. **Just do it!**

Dating yourself heightens your awareness of what you consider fun. This time allows you to gain control of your likes and dislikes. This will also assist you when going on a date with another person.

For years I would accept date invitations to the movies. I could never understand why I would say *"yes"* knowing I was going to fall asleep as soon as the lights were out. I would try to prepare myself early in the day by taking a nap. It was not until I began to date myself did I realize the movies was not somewhere I wanted to be for one and a half to two hours, especially in the dark.

On my dates alone I would, unknowingly, avoid the movies like the plague. One day I said to myself, *"I am going to the movies."* I got online, chose the movie and time then I headed out. When I got there I purchased my ticket, got popcorn and a drink and sat down to be amused. As soon as the lights went out I said to myself *"I do not want to be here."* It was like the lightbulb came on. I got up and left.

It materialized in an instant. I do not like the movie theater. I figured, I never left before because I was with someone else and did not want to seem rude. That experience has inspired me to say *"no"* to movie date requests. Now, that does not mean

I will never go to another movie. It just means if there are other options I will probably choose them.

The point of the matter is had I never dated myself I would have continued to torture myself by doing something I dreaded. It is the simple things in life we need to learn to pay attention to. It is the simple things that make us happy or sad.

Writing #9
- ✓ List days and times you will schedule your dates.
- ✓ List places you will go.
- ✓ List things you want to do.
- ✓ Write a letter to yourself explaining why your dates are important to you.
- ✓ Later in your process write some things you learned about yourself.

_____

_____

_____

Love Yourself

Part II

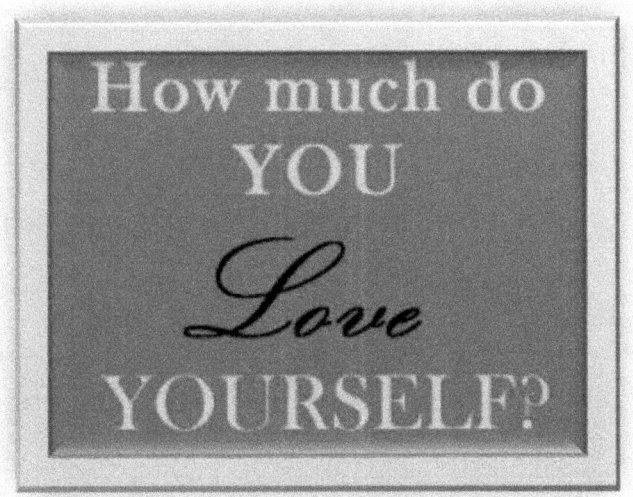

Love yourself enough to encourage yourself. You must be your number one cheerleader. Sure, you may have others who support you, but you are the only one that is with you 100 percent of the time. No one knows you better than you. Speak positivity to yourself. Do not wait for others to plant those seeds.

<u>Writing #10</u>

- ✓ Write an encouraging letter to yourself.

_____

_____

_____

_____

_____

_____

_____

_____

Love yourself enough to know when to walk away. There are times when you may linger in relationships or continue to embrace tasks when you know you need to walk away, if only for a while. Staying does not prove anything to anyone. Continuing involvement in a bad situation may cause resentment which is worse in the end.

Knowing when you cannot do anything else is a part of knowing yourself. When you have done all you know to do in any given situation, I encourage you to walk away. Will it be easy? Will it resolve all the issues at hand? Probably not. Nonetheless, you owe it to yourself to regroup, clear your head and think so you will know what you want your next move to be.

Writing #11

- ✓ Write down situations need to walk away from.
- ✓ What keeps you from doing so?
- ✓ What would happen if you did walk away?

Love yourself enough to take care of yourself emotionally. Any time you go through change your emotions will change. Whether you acknowledge it or not does not mean it is not taking place. It also does not mean the emotions will go away.

You must deal with your emotions. Do not adapt the attitude of *"I'll be alright"* be your escape. Address how you feel and why you feel the way you do. Your emotions/feelings are valid.

Do not take the chance of sweeping your emotions under the rug. If you do, you will risk the possibility of exploding at the wrong time; at the wrong person; and for the wrong reasons.

You can nurture yourself and your emotions in various ways. You can listen to music, exercise, work on a hobby or help others in need.

As you release the negative energy, you create room for positive energy to enter.

Writing #12

- ✓ List five negative emotions you feel often.
- ✓ List ways you can change those feelings.
- ✓ Going forward journal these emotions and how you deal with them.

_____
_____
_____
_____
_____
_____
_____
_____
_____
_____
_____
_____
_____

Love yourself enough to take care of yourself mentally. Change can be stressful. Maximal mental stability helps in easing some of the stress during your change process. No matter the source, stress must be handled in a productive manner.

In December 2003, I became an introvert. I held everything on the inside. I rarely prayed and I stopped going to church. As a result, my mental capacity grossly diminished. I was confused and felt as if I was losing my mind. I did not know how to deal with all the thoughts that seemed to never cease.

I missed an entire year of my life. I checked out mentally. I am not sure how my children were cared for or how I went to work or to school. My reality was so overwhelming that I chose to go elsewhere in my head. *"Have you ever felt that way?"*

January 2005, I decided to fight for my life. I needed to regain control of my atmosphere. After returning to regularly studying the word of God, I made the choice to be an overcomer instead of a victim. I started facing issues in my life head on. With prayer and a strong spiritual support system I became mentally stronger. It took three long years before I realized I was in the beginning stages of my change process.

I chose to read the Bible and other spiritual books for my inner strength. However, there are other ways you can nurture your mentality such as reading your favorite books, journaling your thoughts or meditating daily (Yoga or Pilates) to name a few.

Love yourself enough to take care of yourself physically, including sexually. Your overall health is imperative for longevity of life. You must eat healthier foods, get checkups regularly and partake in some form of physical exercise. When you choose a healthier lifestyle you will notice how much less stressed you feel. This is not an easy change but it can be fun.

If you choose activities that you enjoy such as dancing, running or walking, it will seem less like exercise and more like a pastime. Choose healthful and implement portion control and other options of cooking such as baking, searing or roasting instead of frying.

When it comes to sex, if at all possible, practice celibacy. If not, always protect yourself. There are many sexually transmitted diseases in the world that can change your life forever. When you truly love yourself, you will cherish your body as a gift; meant to be unwrapped by a predestined receiver.

Sex is a rarely resisted human function. Unfortunately, for many of us, this thought is being shared a tad bit late. However, it is never too late to change. If you are not married you should seriously consider this lifestyle change. When you are able to successfully practice abstinence, your level of self-control will be catapulted.

Love yourself enough to take care of yourself spiritually. Humans are spiritual beings. Your spirit is the center of your being. Your spirit controls your mind and your mind controls your body. It is impossible to nurture your body, emotions and mind and neglect your spirit. You must care for your spirit man. **No exceptions.**

Schedule time to pray, read and study regularly. Choose reading materials that you enjoy by authors who interest you. Meditation is also an effective means to sustain your spirit man. It creates one-on-one time with you and the creator.

Love yourself enough to not lower your expectations/standards. You must set expectations /standards for yourself. Do not lower them for anything or anyone. When you lower your expectations/standards you settle for less than you truly deserve. You know what you want. If it is not provided as expected, move on.

Love yourself enough to say *"no"* and be okay with it. Stop allowing others to dictate what you will or will not do. You must stay balanced. To do this, in some instances you must say *"no"*. It is okay to say *"no"* to people when you do not feel like or do not want to do something. Do not feel guilty about it. You have the right to do so. However, when you do things out of love it is different. Saying *"no"* effectively takes practice. As time goes on you will get better at it. Always remember you will never please everyone so when you say *"no"*, say it gracefully.

Writing #13

- ✓ List five things you say **YES** to but in your heart you do not want to do.
- ✓ In a mirror or with someone - practice saying **NO** to each of these things.

_____

_____

_____

Love yourself enough to follow your dreams. A dream is your imagination with no action. Start working toward what you want to be and do. Map out your dream on paper. Set some attainable goals that move you in the direction of completion. Goals are your roadmap for each level of your dream. Surround yourself with others that are focused on accomplishing lifelong dreams and goals.

Search for new opportunities that challenge you to reach for the stars. Search for better ways to perfect your dream. Attend seminars, workshops and other gatherings that will push you to master your skills.

You may lose some friends and family on the way. However, if they are not encouraging you to move full speed ahead are they worth keeping around?

Pursue your dreams and goals in spite of fear. Do it afraid. Do it with a positive attitude. Be enthusiastic and stay focused. You can do it! Never give up!

Writing #14

- ✓ What are your dreams?
- ✓ What is your plan to make them come true?
- ✓ What goals move you toward your dream?

_____

_____

_____

_____

_____

_____

_____

_____

_____

_____

_____

_____

A Note On Love

Love is bigger than you and I. Love covers a multitude of wrongs and rights. We can allow love to come to us but we cannot dictate how, when and where it expresses itself. We can surrender to love or not, but, in the end, it strikes suddenly. It's unpredictable and unnervingly clear. Sometimes we even find ourselves loving people we don't even like. Love comes with no conditions or stipulations. It is like the moon in the night: it shines regardless of our fears and desires.

Depending on the relationship, loving someone else can be scary. Love causes us to be vulnerable and it causes us to take a risk. When we think of vulnerability we instantly think weakness. When we think of risk, we think of fear. And honestly, no one wants to be vulnerable or take risks with their hearts.

However, when dealing with love, vulnerability and risks simply allow us to open our hearts to natural emotions and feelings. It allows us to be able to receive what others freely give - Love.

Love cannot be turned on as a reward. It cannot be turned off as a punishment nor can it be bought. Real love produces tangible actions and it requires a lot of effort. Love cannot dwell in selfishness. Love is a requirement on this earth.

Love is attainable by all who pursue it. I pray you enjoy the experience of learning to fully Love Yourself. You deserve the best. You should give yourself the best of you and it starts with inner LOVE!

SPEAK LIFE!!
Declare and decree over your life daily...
I AM courageous.
I AM determined.
I AM unstoppable.
I AM victorious.
I AM love.
I AM gifted.
I AM anointed.
I AM blessed.
I AM successful.
I AM healed.
I AM beautiful.
I AM whole.
I AM confident.
I AM forgiving.
I AM grateful.
I AM generous
I AM strengthened.
I AM well-able
I AM favored.
I AM God's masterpiece.